How To Train Your

Basset Hound

An Expert Guide to Smart Socialization Strategies for Caring, Grooming, and Raising a confident Hunting dog

Finnley Crestwood

How to Train your

Basset Hound

Contents

Introduction

If you're the proud owner of a Basset Hound, or are considering adding one of these adorable, low-slung pups to your family, you're in for a real treat. Basset Hounds are truly one-of-a-kind dogs - their distinctive long bodies, short legs, and soulful eyes have captured the hearts of dog lovers for generations. But beneath that irresistible exterior lies a breed that can be as stubborn as they are affectionate, making training a unique challenge.

As a lifelong dog enthusiast, I know this firsthand. Several years ago, I brought home a rambunctious Basset Hound puppy named Rufus, and let me tell you, training him was no easy feat. Rufus had a mind of his own and seemed to selectively ignore my commands, often getting distracted by the slightest scent or smallest movement. I quickly learned that the key to successfully training a

Basset Hound involves patience, positivity, and a deep understanding of this unique breed.

Through countless training sessions, trial and error, and a whole lot of canine-approved treats, I was eventually able to transform Rufus into a well-behaved, obedient companion. Today, he's the pride of our neighborhood, greeting everyone he meets with a wagging tail and an infectious zest for life. But it wasn't always that way – Rufus and I had to overcome some serious hurdles to get to where we are now.

That's why I'm thrilled to share with you the strategies and techniques I developed for training my Basset Hound. In this comprehensive guide, you'll discover the secrets to unlocking your Basset's full potential, from mastering basic obedience commands to tackling more advanced behaviors. Whether you're a first-time Basset Hound owner or a seasoned pro, you'll find invaluable insights that will help you build a strong, trusting bond with your canine companion.

So, what makes the Basset Hound such a unique and captivating breed? For starters, their long, low-to-the-ground bodies were bred for hunting, with a keen sense of smell that can rival even the most sophisticated search-and-rescue dogs. These lovable pups were originally used to track small prey, like rabbits and hares, thanks to their exceptional olfactory abilities and stamina.

But don't let their hunting heritage fool you — Basset Hounds are also renowned for their affectionate, gentle nature. They thrive on human companionship and make wonderful family pets, greeting everyone they meet with a wagging tail and soulful eyes. With their characteristic droopy ears, wrinkled faces, and big, brown eyes, it's no wonder Basset Hounds have become such beloved icons in popular culture.

However, this breed's unique characteristics can also present some training challenges. Basset Hounds are notoriously independent and can be quite stubborn, often choosing to ignore commands in favor of following their noses. Their low-to-the-ground stature and natural instinct to sniff the ground can make basic obedience training, like teaching the "heel" command, a real test of patience and perseverance.

But fear not, fellow Basset Hound enthusiasts! With the right approach and a deep understanding of your canine companion's needs, you can overcome these obstacles and transform your Basset into a well-mannered, obedient partner. In the pages that follow, you'll discover the secrets to successful Basset Hound training, from establishing a consistent routine and mastering positive reinforcement techniques to tackling advanced commands and troubleshooting common behavioral issues.

Get ready to embark on an exciting journey with your Basset Hound, where every training session is an opportunity to deepen your bond and unleash your dog's full potential. With the guidance and proven strategies in this book, you'll be well on your way to raising a happy, healthy, and exceptionally well-trained Basset Hound. So, let's get started!

Chapter One

Understanding the Basset Hound

Basset Hound Personality and Temperament

Famous for their endearing dispositions and unusual appearance, Basset Hounds are a one-of-a-kind dog breed. These stocky hounds have evolved from their hunting roots into cherished pets and members of the family. To train and bond with these loving dogs, it is essential to understand the Basset Hound's temperament and personality.

The Basset Hound is easily recognizable by its calm demeanor and lack of energy. These dogs usually do not get excited about much and would rather spend the day lounging about the house. Because they are neither hyperactive nor easily stressed, they are great companions for families or anyone who wants something low-key. Another characteristic of Basset Hounds is their kind and loving nature, which allows them to develop deep attachments to their human families.

Basset Hounds are known for their placid nature, but they are not afraid to get into trouble or be defiant. Without the right kind of training and socialization, their natural hunting drive and strong sense of independence can cause them to run away or disregard your orders. Basset Hounds can be highly determined, and their innate tendency to follow their noses can occasionally get them into trouble. It is crucial to create early training and provide positive reinforcement to help curb any undesired tendencies.

Another noticeable element of the Basset Hound's personality is its vocalness. These hounds are recognized for their characteristic baying or howling, which they utilize to communicate and convey their feelings. While this behavior can be appealing, it is crucial to handle excessive barking or screaming through adequate training and socialization.

Overall, the Basset Hound's demeanor is a unique blend of laid-back devotion, mischievousness, and vocal expressiveness. Understanding and embracing these features is crucial to creating a successful and happy relationship with these adorable canines.

Basset Hound Physical Characteristics and Needs

Basset Hounds are readily recognizable by their distinctive physical traits, which have been meticulously honed over centuries of selective breeding. These short-legged, long-bodied hounds exhibit a distinct collection of qualities that not only contribute to their appealing appearance but also determine their specific needs and care requirements.

One of the most noticeable qualities of the Basset Hound is their low-to-the-ground posture. Standing about 12 to 15 inches tall at the shoulder, these dogs are recognized for their short, powerful legs and elongated bodies. This particular build is the product of a hereditary disorder called chondrodysplasia, which causes the Basset Hound's long bones to stop growing at a specific point, resulting in their distinguishing appearance.

While the Basset Hound's physical traits may be extremely pleasing, they also present some particular issues. The breed's long back and low-to-the-ground attitude can leave them susceptible to back and joint problems, particularly as they age. It is crucial to provide Basset Hounds with proper exercise, maintain a healthy weight, and avoid activities that impose excessive strain on their spine and joints.

In addition to their physical build, Basset Hounds are also noted for their remarkable facial traits, including large, pendulous ears and a slightly furrowed brow. These traits not only contribute to the breed's attractive appearance but also serve practical advantages. The Basset Hound's big, floppy ears help to catch scent particles and aid in their hunting ability, while the wrinkled brow may help to protect their eyes from pollution and environmental threats.

Another major physical attribute of the Basset Hound is its dense, short-haired coat. While these dogs do not require considerable care, their coat does shed considerably, and regular brushing is recommended to help remove loose hair and keep a healthy coat and skin.

When it comes to the Basset Hound's exercise and activity needs, these dogs are normally pleased with moderate, low-impact exercises. Due to their physical build and inclination to be prone to joint and back ailments, Basset Hounds should not engage in high-impact exercises or extended, rigorous activity. Instead, they thrive on daily walks, recreation in a secure, fenced-in area, and mental stimulation through training and puzzle toys.

By understanding the Basset Hound's specific physical qualities and needs, owners can guarantee that their cherished companions stay healthy, happy, and comfortable throughout their lives.

Establishing a Positive Bond with Your Basset Hound

Developing a strong, positive link between a Basset Hound and their human companion is vital for successful training, socialization, and overall well-being. These friendly and loyal dogs rely on the love and attention of their family, and by taking the time to form a meaningful relationship, owners can create a foundation for a rewarding and lasting alliance.

One of the most crucial aspects of building a healthy attachment with a Basset Hound is to focus on quality time and positive reinforcement. These dogs are frequently eager to please and respond well to praise, affection, and prizes. Dedicating regular moments of focused playtime, training, and cuddling can assist in building the bond and convey to the Basset Hound that their person is a reliable source of comfort and happiness.

It is also vital to approach training and socializing with patience and persistence. Basset Hounds can be independent and stubborn at times, and unexpected or harsh training methods can break the trust and attachment between the dog and its owner. Instead, employ positive reinforcement approaches, such as clicker training or reward-based methods, to encourage desired actions and develop the Basset Hound's confidence and readiness to comply.

In addition to training, providing mental and physical stimulation can also aid in deepening the bond between a Basset Hound and their owner. These dogs thrive on activities that test their problem-solving skills and stimulate their innate hunting instincts, such as scent work, nose games, and puzzle toys. By incorporating these enriching activities into the everyday routine, owners can establish a greater sense of trust and cooperation with their Basset Hound.

It is also crucial to be cognizant of the Basset Hound's demand for affection and company. These canines are generally prone to separation anxiety and can become agitated when left alone for extended periods. By providing numerous opportunities for cuddles, belly rubs, and one-on-one attention, owners may help to reassure their Basset Hound and build the link between them.

Ultimately, creating a solid bond with a Basset Hound involves a combination of patience, persistence, and a real desire to understand and meet the specific requirements of these lovable canines. By prioritizing the relationship and fostering a compassionate, supportive atmosphere, owners can create a strong and enduring connection with their Basset Hound that will enrich both of their lives.

Chapter Two

Preparing for Training

Gathering the Right Training Supplies

Successful Basset Hound training begins with obtaining the right resources and equipment. Equipping yourself with the required gear not only helps to assure the efficacy of your training sessions but also contributes to the overall well-being and safety of your canine companion. From basic obedience to more sophisticated tactics, the correct training supplies can make all the difference in reaching your intended training goals.

One of the most necessary accessories for Basset Hound training is a high-quality leash and harness.

Given the breed's low-to-the-ground height and tendency to be independent, a tight and comfortable leash and harness system is vital for keeping control during training and ordinary walks. Look for a lightweight, adjustable harness that distributes pressure equally across the Basset Hound's chest and shoulders, rather than the neck, to reduce strain or discomfort. A robust, six-foot leash with a comfortable grasp can offer the required control while still allowing your Basset Hound some freedom of mobility.

In addition to the leash and harness, the use of positive reinforcement tools, including biscuits and clickers, can substantially assist the training process. Basset Hounds are generally highly food-motivated, making small, bite-sized training treats an ideal reward for desired behaviors. When purchasing snacks, look for nutritious, natural products that are low in fat and high in protein to promote your Basset Hound's overall health. Clickers, on the other hand, can be a valuable tool in clicker training, as they allow you to precisely note the exact instant your Basset Hound accomplishes the desired behavior, reinforcing the connection between the action and the reward.

Another key training supply to consider is a comfortable, defined training location or surface. This might be a specialized room in your home, a fenced-in yard, or a peaceful public area, depending on the type of training you're working on. Ensure that the training area is free from distractions, has a non-slip surface, and provides a safe, controlled atmosphere for your Basset Hound to focus on the task at hand.

For more advanced training, such as agility or scent work, you may need to invest in additional specialized equipment, such as agility obstacles, scent kits, or puzzle toys. These types of training tools can serve to challenge your Basset Hound's problem-solving skills, provide mental stimulation, and improve the link between you and your canine partner.

Finally, it's necessary to have a dependable way of capturing and documenting your Basset Hound's training progress, such as a training notebook or a smartphone camera. Keeping note of your dog's triumphs, problems, and training milestones will allow you to alter your strategy, recognize successes, and stay motivated throughout the training process.

By carefully selecting and preparing the correct training supplies, you can create a good, efficient, and pleasurable training experience for both you and your Basset Hound, creating the foundation for a well-trained and confident canine partner.

Creating a Consistent Training Environment

Establishing a regular training environment is vital for the success of your Basset Hound's training. These loyal, yet occasionally independent-minded, dogs thrive on discipline and predictability, and by setting a well-defined training schedule and area, you may help your Basset Hound feel secure, focused, and more responsive to your instructions.

One of the first steps in developing a regular training environment is to designate a specific area or room in your home as the primary training place. This specific training environment should be free from distractions, such as high-traffic zones, other pets, or loud noises, allowing your Basset Hound to focus exclusively on the task at hand. Consider setting up the space with non-slip flooring, soft mats or blankets, and any essential training equipment, such as a leash, treats, and clickers.

Consistency in the training environment also extends to the schedule and organization of your training sessions. Establishing a regular plan, such as training for 10-15 minutes every morning or evening, might assist your Basset Hound in anticipating and preparing for the training process. This consistent pattern not only promotes the value of training but also helps to decrease any fear or confusion your Basset Hound may suffer.

In addition to a steady timetable, it's crucial to keep a calm and cheerful tone throughout the training sessions. Basset Hounds are sensitive to their human emotions and can pick up on any dissatisfaction or impatience, which might impair the training process. Approach each session with a patient, encouraging attitude, and be careful of your body language and voice cues, as they can substantially affect your Basset Hound's readiness to interact and learn.

Another crucial part of creating a consistent training environment is the engagement of all family members. Ensure that everyone who interacts with your Basset Hound, from children to other adults, understands and follows the same training standards and orders. This constancy encourages the appropriate behaviors and prevents your Basset Hound from becoming confused or developing selective obedience.

Finally, be cautious of any changes or disturbances to your Basset Hound's training environment, since these might impair their learning and confidence. If you need to modify the training space or routine, introduce the changes gradually and provide adequate reassurance and positive reinforcement to help your canine partner adapt.

By establishing a consistent training environment, complete with a designated space, predictable timetable, and positive reinforcement, you can create a setting that is conducive to your Basset

Hound's learning and assist in building a foundation of trust, confidence, and obedience.

Identifying Positive Reinforcements for Your Basset Hound

Positive reinforcement is a cornerstone of successful Basset Hound training since these friendly and typically food-motivated pups respond extraordinarily well to prizes and praise. By identifying and successfully employing positive reinforcements, you can not only speed up your Basset Hound's learning process but also enhance the link between you and your furry buddy.

One of the most prevalent and effective positive reinforcements for Basset Hounds is food-based treats. These hounds are typically highly motivated by the prospect of a tasty reward, making small, bite-sized treats an effective tool for reinforcing desired behaviors during training sessions. When selecting snacks, consider items that are healthful, low in fat, and high in protein, such as small pieces of cooked chicken, freeze-dried meat, or specially developed training treats.

It's vital to remember that the type and frequency of goodies used during training should be carefully assessed. Overfeeding can lead to weight gain and other health issues, so it's crucial to portion the treats carefully and use them judiciously as a reinforcement, rather than a primary food source. Additionally, you may want to experiment with different treatment varieties to establish your Basset Hound's unique preferences and what works best to stimulate them during training.

In addition to food-based rewards, many Basset Hounds also respond positively to praise and affection as positive reinforcements. These sensitive dogs thrive on the attention and praise of their human companions, and a simple "good boy" or a soft pat can be just as helpful as a treat in reinforcing desired actions. Incorporate plenty of verbal praising, stroking, and other types of physical affection into your training sessions to establish the connection between your Basset Hound's activities and your positive response.

For more advanced training or to provide more mental stimulation, you might also consider using toys or interactive games as positive incentives. Basset Hounds generally like engaging in activities that challenge their problem-solving skills, such as snuffle mats, puzzle toys, or scent-based games. By combining these types of reinforcements into your training, you may create a more well-rounded and enriching experience for your canine friend.

It's crucial to remember that the specific positive incentives that work best for your Basset Hound may vary, as each dog is an individual with unique preferences and motivations. Observe your Basset Hound's reactions throughout training and be open to experimenting with different rewards to learn what works best for your dog.

By identifying and properly implementing positive reinforcements, you can create a training environment that is exciting, engaging, and beneficial for both you and your Basset Hound. This technique not only helps to quicken the learning process but also builds a strong, trusting bond between you and your canine partner.

Chapter Three

Basic Obedience Training

Teaching the "Sit," "Stay," and "Come" Commands

Establishing a firm foundation in basic obedience training is vital for any Basset Hound owner, as these instructions create the foundations for a well-behaved and attentive canine partner. Among the most crucial basic commands are "sit," "stay," and "come," each of which serves a specific purpose in helping to assure your Basset Hound's safety and compliance.

The "sit" command is one of the core obedience signals and an ideal beginning point for Basset Hound training. Teaching your Basset Hound to sit on command not only helps to establish your place as the leader but also provides a reliable means to regulate your dog's behavior in numerous situations, such as welcoming visitors or waiting patiently for their meals.

To teach the "sit" command, begin by holding a treat close to your Basset Hound's nose and slowly sliding it back towards their shoulders, causing them to naturally sit as they follow the reward. As your Basset Hound's rump meets the ground, quickly say the cue "sit" and reward them with the treat and plenty of praise. Repeat this method multiple times during each training session, progressively increasing the duration your Basset Hound holds the sit position before earning the reward.

The "stay" command is another key basic obedience ability, as it trains your Basset Hound to remain in a certain position until released. This command is particularly effective in instances where you require your dog to wait, such as before crossing a street or when welcoming guests. Start by having your Basset Hound sit or lie down, then take a step back while delivering the "stay" cue. If your dog remains in position, give them a treat and praise. Gradually increase the distance and duration of the "stay" over numerous training sessions, always releasing your Basset Hound with a specific word or phrase, such as "okay" or "all done."

The "come" order is possibly one of the most crucial basic obedience abilities, as it can be a lifeline in emergencies. Teaching your Basset Hound to reliably return to you when called is crucial for their safety and your peace of mind. Begin by grabbing your Basset Hound's attention, using food or a toy to pull them towards you while saying the "come" cue. As they reach you, thank them with the goodie and warm praise. Gradually increase the distance and distractions during your training sessions, always rewarding your Basset Hound for a good recall.

It's vital to note that constant repetition and patience are key while teaching these fundamental commands to your Basset Hound. These hounds can be independent-minded and may require more time and repetition to completely grasp the abilities. Utilizing positive reinforcement strategies, like food, praise, and clicker training, can dramatically increase the learning process and assist in building your Basset Hound's confidence and motivation.

Furthermore, it's crucial to practice these fundamental commands in a range of circumstances, from the comfort of your home to more distracting public settings. This exposure helps to guarantee that your Basset Hound's obedience abilities are reliable and adaptable to real-world circumstances.

By routinely training and reinforcing the "sit," "stay," and "come" commands, you can develop a firm foundation of obedience that will serve as a springboard for more advanced training and assist in keeping your Basset Hound safe and well-behaved in several circumstances.

Introducing the "Down" and "Roll Over" Commands

Building upon the core obedience abilities of "sit," "stay," and "come," the "down" and "roll over" commands offer additional layers of control and variety in your Basset Hound's training. These more complex cues not only indicate your Basset Hound's level of training but also provide vital possibilities for bonding, mental stimulation, and reinforcing positive behaviors.

The "down" command teaches your Basset Hound to lie down on the ground, a helpful skill in numerous settings, such as when welcoming guests, resting on a stroll, or when you need your dog to remain in a calm, submissive position. To teach the "down" command, start by having your Basset Hound in a sitting position and hold a treat close to their nose. Slowly lower the treat towards the ground, guiding your dog's body into a lying down position. As they lower themselves, say the cue "down" and reward them with the goodie and praise. Gradually increase the duration your Basset Hound holds the "down" position before obtaining the prize.

The "roll over" command, while not strictly a practical ability for everyday life, can be a wonderful trick that highlights your Basset Hound's training and willingness to engage with you. This order also provides an opportunity for enhanced mental stimulation and physical engagement, as it challenges your Basset Hound to move their body in a novel way.

To teach the "roll over" command, begin by having your Basset Hound in the "down" position. Hold a reward close to their nose and slowly transfer it from one side of their body to the other, encouraging them to swivel their head and finally roll their body over to follow the treat. As they accomplish the roll, say the cue "roll over" and reward them with the treat and praise. Gradually increase the distance and time of the roll, always praising your Basset Hound for their progress.

It's crucial to note that the "roll over" command may be more problematic for some Basset Hounds, as their long backs and low-to-the-ground stature can make the movement less comfortable or natural for them. Be patient, listen to your dog's body language, and never force them to perform the behavior if they look uncomfortable or distressed.

As with the other fundamental obedience commands, constant repetition and positive reinforcement are crucial to success while teaching the "down" and "roll over" cues. Incorporate these commands into your normal training sessions, gradually increasing the difficulty and duration, and be sure to celebrate your Basset Hound's achievements with enthusiastic praise and incentives.

By mastering the "down" and "roll over" commands, you not only enhance your Basset Hound's repertoire of obedience abilities but also deepen the link between you and your canine partner. These advanced signs reflect your dog's willingness to trust and cooperate with you, creating the foundation for a solid, lasting connection built on mutual understanding and respect.

Mastering the "Heel" and "Leave It" Commands

As your Basset Hound develops through their basic obedience training, introducing the "heel" and "leave it" commands can assist to further polish their behavior and prepare them for navigating the world with confidence and safety.

The "heel" order instructs your Basset Hound to walk closely by your side, rather than dragging or roaming ahead. This talent is extremely important while traversing crowded locations, crossing streets, or simply having a stroll together. To teach the "heel" command, begin by having your Basset Hound on a loose leash on your left side. Reward them with a treat and praise anytime they remain in the proper heel posture, and progressively increase the duration and distance of the heel behavior throughout numerous training sessions.

It's crucial to remember that teaching the "heel" command may be more problematic for Basset Hounds since their independent character and strong hunting instincts might make them prone to yanking on the leash. Be patient, employ positive reinforcement tactics, and consider the use of a front-clipping harness or head halter to provide additional control and guidance during the training process.

The "leave it" command, on the other hand, trains your Basset Hound to ignore or disengage from an item or circumstance that may be tempting or hazardous. This talent is particularly important when navigating situations with possible risks, such as discarded food, small items, or unknown animals. To teach the "leave it" command, begin by laying a treat on the ground and covering it with your hand. When your Basset Hound approaches and shows curiosity, say "leave it" and reward them with a different treat from your other hand when they turn away. Gradually raise the difficulty by laying the treat on the ground and only rewarding your Basset Hound when they entirely disengage from it.

Mastering the "heel" and "leave it" commands not only enhances your Basset Hound's loyalty and safety but also displays their degree of training and your commitment to responsible pet management. These advanced talents can be particularly beneficial when navigating public settings, dealing with other people and animals, or meeting unexpected events throughout your regular activities.

As with all obedience training, constant repetition, patience, and positive reinforcement are vital to success. Be prepared to alter your training approach to meet your Basset Hound's specific personality and learning style, and applaud their accomplishments along the way.

By including the "heel" and "leave it" commands into your Basset Hound's training regimen, you can equip your canine partner with the skills and confidence needed to navigate the world safely and responsibly, while building the link between you and your beloved dog.

Chapter Four

Potty Training Your Basset Hound

Understanding Basset Hound Potty Habits

Effective toilet training is a key element of responsible Basset Hound ownership. These loyal, yet often stubborn, hounds require patience and consistency when it comes to training good elimination habits. Understanding the particular toilet habits of the Basset Hound breed is the first step towards successful potty training and a clean, well-behaved canine partner.

Basset Hounds are generally a clean breed, but their low-to-the-ground height and natural desire to follow their noses can often make potty training challenging. These hounds have a rather high metabolism and may need to relieve themselves more frequently than some other breeds, particularly during the puppy stage.

One of the essential elements to consider while potty training a Basset Hound is their natural desire to excrete in areas with strong scent indicators. Basset Hounds are recognized for their great sense of smell, and they may be lured to spots where they or other animals have previously discharged themselves. This can make it difficult to develop a consistent bathroom schedule, as your Basset Hound may attempt to return to familiar, but inappropriate, excretion areas.

Additionally, Basset Hounds might be subject to submissive urine, a behavior commonly seen in response to perceived threats or high-stress circumstances. This can manifest during training, when greeting new people or animals, or when being scolded. Understanding and managing submissive urination is a crucial element of successful Basset Hound potty training.

Another particular attribute of the Basset Hound that can affect toilet training is their predisposition to be independent-minded and occasionally stubborn. These hounds may be less sensitive to typical training methods, needing a more patient and positive reinforcement-based approach to attain the required results.

By taking the time to study the individual toilet habits and behavioral patterns of the Basset Hound breed, you can personalize your potty training method to better meet your canine companion's needs. This understanding will not only help you achieve a successful outcome but also develop a stronger, more trustworthy bond between you and your Basset Hound.

Establishing a Potty Schedule and Routine

Establishing a consistent potty training schedule and routine is vital for successfully housebreaking your Basset Hound. These friendly, yet occasionally independent-minded, hounds thrive on structure and regularity, and by developing a well-defined toilet routine, you may help your Basset Hound understand when and where it is proper to excrete.

One of the first tasks in designing a potty training regimen is to determine your Basset Hound's normal excretion patterns. Pay close attention to your dog's behavior, such as sniffing, circling, or demonstrating restlessness, as these can be indicators that they need to go potty. Maintain a journal of when your Basset Hound generally has to relieve themselves, taking note of any patterns or triggers that may influence their potty habits.

Armed with this information, you can next develop a consistent toilet training timetable that coincides with your Basset Hound's natural rhythms. Aim to take your dog out to their designated pee place at regular intervals, such as first thing in the morning, after meals, after playtime or naps, and before sleep. Consistency is crucial, as it helps your Basset Hound anticipate and prepare for their bathroom breaks, lowering the likelihood of accidents.

In addition to a constant schedule, providing a designated potty place is also vital for successful Basset Hound potty training. Choose an outdoor place that is easily accessible, free from distractions, and routinely used for this purpose. Accompany your Basset Hound to this spot each time they need to go, using a specific verbal cue, such as "go potty," to reinforce the relationship between the location and the desired activity.

Rewarding your Basset Hound with praise, rewards, and affection immediately after they excrete in the appropriate place is a vital component of building a successful potty training program. This positive reinforcement helps to cement the connection between the desired behavior and the reward, making it more likely that your Basset Hound will repeat the action in the future.

It's crucial to note that the duration of the potty training procedure can vary depending on your Basset Hound's age, disposition, and previous experiences. Puppies and freshly adopted Basset Hounds may require more frequent outdoor outings and tighter monitoring to minimize accidents, while older, previously trained dogs may adapt more readily to a new routine.

Throughout the potty training adventure, be patient, consistent, and attentive to your Basset Hound's requirements. Celebrate little wins, such as successful bathroom sessions, and be prepared to change your approach if you experience any problems or setbacks. By developing a well-defined potty training timetable and routine, you may help your Basset Hound become a well-behaved, house-trained companion.

Addressing and Preventing Potty Accidents

Despite your best efforts, toilet training your Basset Hound may not always go as well as intended. Accidents may and will happen, and it's crucial to have a plan in place to manage them properly and prevent future occurrences.

One of the major tactics for resolving bathroom accidents is to remain calm and tolerant. Basset Hounds are sensitive to their owner's emotions, and a harsh or punishing response can break the trust and bond between you and your canine partner. Instead, focus on gently retraining your Basset Hound to their designated potty spot and providing good praise when they are eliminated in the appropriate location.

If you catch your Basset Hound in the act of having an accident, immediately interrupt the activity with a stern "no" or "ah-ah" and quickly accompany them to their potty location. Avoid the temptation to rub their nose in the muck, as this method is not only unproductive but can also be damaging to your Basset Hound's well-being and training progress.

After the mishap, carefully clean the area with an enzymatic cleanser designed to remove pet odors. This helps to eliminate any remaining scent cues that may bring your Basset Hound back to the same location, encouraging unwanted behavior.

In instances where you notice a potty accident after the fact, it's crucial not to penalize or scold your Basset Hound, since they will not be able to establish the connection between the past behavior and the current outcome. Instead, focus on cleaning the area, emphasizing the right potty pattern, and being more vigilant in the future.

Preventing toilet accidents is a key element of successful Basset Hound potty training. This includes attentively monitoring your dog's behavior and providing them with adequate opportunities to excrete in the appropriate spot.

One helpful technique for minimizing accidents is to increase the frequency of outdoor bathroom breaks, especially for puppies and newly adopted Basset Hounds. These dogs may have smaller bladders and less control over their excretion behaviors, necessitating more frequent treks to their allotted pee place.

Crate training can also be a great aid in preventing potty accidents, as Basset Hounds normally do not want to pollute their dwelling space. When used appropriately, a crate can help educate your dog to contain their bladder and intestines until they are released to their potty location.

Additionally, be cautious of any environmental or situational triggers that may contribute to toilet accidents, such as stress, excitement, or changes in routine. By anticipating these triggers and making early efforts to prevent accidents, you can reinforce your Basset Hound's healthy potty habits and limit the danger of setbacks.

Addressing and preventing potty accidents involves patience, consistency, and a deep understanding of your Basset Hound's individual needs and tendencies. By approaching these problems with a positive, sympathetic attitude, you may help your canine companion become a well-trained, house-trained member of your family.

Chapter Five

Leash Training

Introducing the Leash and Harness

Leash training is an essential component of responsible Basset Hound ownership, as it not only assures the safety and well-being of your canine friend but also helps to develop a foundation of control and trust. Introducing the leash and harness to your Basset Hound in a nice, gradual manner is the first step towards acquiring this crucial ability.

One of the most critical considerations when beginning leash training is the sort of equipment you purchase. Basset Hounds, with their low-to-the-ground size and tendency to be independent-minded, may fare best with a front-clipping harness or a head halter, as these devices offer the operator more control and power over the dog's movements. Traditional collar-and-leash configurations can sometimes encourage pulling and may place unnecessary strain on the Basset Hound's sensitive neck and spine.

When introducing the harness or head halter, take it gradually and allow your Basset Hound to study the new equipment at their own pace. Offer treats and praise as they become acquainted with the feel and appearance of the harness or head halter, gradually acclimating them to the procedure of putting it on and taking it off. This positive association will encourage your Basset Hound to regard the leash and harness as a forerunner to fun activities, rather than a source of tension or discomfort.

Once your Basset Hound is acquainted with the equipment, you may begin the process of introducing the leash. Start by allowing your dog to pull a lightweight leash about the house or yard, providing them with the opportunity to grow used to the sensation and sound of the leash without the extra pressure of being linked to it. Gradually increase the length your Basset Hound wears the leash, delivering goodies and praise whenever they remain quiet and relaxed.

When your Basset Hound is adjusted to the leash, you may begin the process of walking with it attached. Start in a familiar, low-distraction location, such as your backyard or a calm neighborhood street, and leave the leash-free, enabling your Basset Hound to explore without feeling constricted. Whenever your dog maintains a loose, relaxed leash, reward them with praise and food, reinforcing the desirable behavior.

It's crucial to note that the pace of leash training might vary substantially depending on your Basset Hound's specific temperament and prior experiences. Some dogs may take to the technique more readily, while others may require more time and care. Be prepared to adapt your training strategy as needed, always keeping your dog's comfort and well-being at the forefront of your efforts.

By introducing the leash and harness in a pleasant, gradual manner, you can help your Basset Hound create a comfortable, confident relationship with this critical equipment, laying the framework for effective leash training and a well-behaved, obedient canine friend.

Practicing Loose Leash Walking

Mastering the skill of loose leash walking is a vital component of Basset Hound training, as it not only assures the safety and well-being of your canine friend but also enhances the overall enjoyment of your joint walks and adventures. Basset Hounds, with their independent personality and excellent sense of smell, can often be prone to pulling on the leash, making this ability a crucial one to acquire.

The key to teaching your Basset Hound to walk on a loose leash is to promote the desired behavior – a comfortable, attentive pace at your side – through positive reinforcement. Begin by introducing your dog to the concept of loose leash walking in a low-distraction location, such as your backyard or a quiet neighborhood street.

When your Basset Hound is strolling next to you with a loose, relaxed leash, immediately reward them with praise, cookies, or a favorite toy. This positive reinforcement helps to cement the connection between the desired behavior (walking peacefully at your side) and the reward, inspiring your dog to repeat the action.

As your Basset Hound becomes more comfortable with loose leash walking, gradually increase the duration and distance of your training sessions, slowly introducing more distractions and tougher surroundings. This gradual exposure helps to guarantee that your dog's loose leash walking skills are reliable and applicable to real-world circumstances.

One excellent strategy for maintaining a loose leash is the "be a tree" concept. Whenever your Basset Hound tries to tug or wander ahead, stop walking and stand motionless, refusing to move forward until the leash is loose again. This teaches your dog that pushing or forging ahead results in a lack of forward progress, reinforcing the desirable slack leash behavior.

It's vital to understand that Basset Hounds can occasionally be rebellious or independent-minded, which can make loose leash walking a particular hardship. In these circumstances, it may be good to utilize a front-clipping harness or head halter, as these items can offer you greater control and leverage over your dog's motions.

Consistency and patience are crucial when introducing loose-leash walking to your Basset Hound. Celebrate little triumphs, such as your dog keeping a loose leash for a few paces, and be prepared to adapt your training strategy as needed to keep your canine friend involved and motivated.

By learning the art of loose leash walking, you can not only protect the safety and well-being of your Basset Hound but also boost the overall enjoyment of your shared outdoor activities. This vital ability builds the foundation for a well-behaved, obedient canine companion who can confidently navigate the world by your side.

Overcoming Leash Reactivity

Leash reactivity is a typical difficulty faced by Basset Hound owners, as these loyal yet independent-minded hounds can occasionally become overwhelmed or overstimulated when encountering other dogs, people, or environmental triggers when on the leash. Addressing and overcoming leash sensitivity needs a careful, comprehensive approach, but the rewards of a well-trained, confident Basset Hound are well worth the effort.

At the heart of leash reactivity is a combination of fear, excitement, and lack of confidence. Basset Hounds, with their excellent sense of smell and strong hunting drive, may become highly stimulated or agitated when confronted with imagined threats or unexpected stimuli while on the leash, resulting in barking, lunging, or other reactive behaviors.

The first step in resolving leash reactivity is to identify the particular triggers that produce these unpleasant behaviors. Pay special attention to your Basset Hound's body language and energy levels when encountering new people, animals, or environmental elements, and make a note of the scenarios that seem to generate the most worry or excitement.

Once you have identified the trigger points, you can begin to apply a systematic desensitization and counterconditioning strategy. This entails progressively exposing your Basset Hound to the triggers, starting from a distance where they stay calm and comfortable, and matching the exposure with positive reinforcement, such as food or praise.

For example, if your Basset Hound becomes reactive when facing other dogs on the leash, you would begin by having your dog examine other dogs from a distance where they remain calm and focused on you. As your dog remains comfortable, give them goodies and vocal praise. Gradually lower the distance between your dog and the other dogs, always maintaining inside the threshold where your Basset Hound can maintain their composure.

It's crucial to note that the pace of this desensitization process may vary depending on your Basset Hound's specific temperament and level of reactivity. Some dogs may improve more quickly, while others may require more time and patience. Be prepared to change the distance and duration of the exposure as needed to ensure your Basset Hound remains calm and engaged during the training.

In addition to the desensitization regimen, it's also crucial to provide your Basset Hound with adequate opportunities for socialization and confidence-building. Enroll in positive-reinforcement-based obedience training, arrange playdates with well-socialized canine companions, and introduce your dog to a variety of unusual yet non-threatening activities. By boosting your Basset Hound's overall confidence and resilience, you can assist in decreasing the danger of leash reactivity in the long term.

Overcoming leash reactivity in Basset Hounds involves a complex strategy, combining patience, perseverance, and a deep understanding of your dog's specific requirements and triggers. With time, effort, and the appropriate training techniques, you can help your Basset Hound become a calm, confident, and well-behaved companion, both on and off the leash.

Chapter Six

Socialization and Behavior Management

Socializing Your Basset Hound

Socialization is a key element of growing a well-adjusted and well-behaved Basset Hound. These friendly, yet occasionally independent-minded, hounds thrive on good encounters with humans, animals, and new situations, and early and regular socialization can help to minimize the development of fear, anxiety, and other behavioral difficulties.

The socializing process should begin as early as possible, ideally during the important socialization phase, which normally lasts until a Basset Hound reaches 12-16 weeks of age. During this period, it's crucial to introduce your puppy to a wide variety of good experiences, including meeting new people, engaging with other well-socialized dogs, and discovering diverse sights, sounds, and textures.

When exposing your Basset Hound puppy to new people and animals, always ensure that the encounters are calm, regulated, and positive. Provide plenty of goodies, praise, and encouragement to help your puppy associate these experiences with something nice. Avoid forced encounters or situations that may cause your puppy to feel overwhelmed or afraid since these can contribute to the development of long-term behavioral problems.

As your Basset Hound matures, it's crucial to continue the socialization process, gradually introducing them to new activities and surroundings. This may involve taking them on field excursions to pet-friendly establishments, parks, or community events, where they can safely interact with varied groups of people and other animals under your supervision.

When socializing your Basset Hound, it's vital to be sensitive to their body language and energy levels. Some Basset Hounds may be more extroverted and confident, while others may be more reserved or bashful. Respect your dog's comfort zone and never force them into circumstances that bring them grief. Instead, utilize positive reinforcement to gradually improve their confidence and willingness to interact with new situations.

In addition to in-person socialization, you can also incorporate virtual or remote socialization possibilities, such as video conversations with friends and family members, or even "virtual" playdates with other dog owners. These types of interactions can help to increase your Basset Hound's social circle while keeping a safe, controlled setting.

Proper socialization not only helps to prevent behavioral difficulties but also enriches your Basset Hound's life by equipping them with the confidence and skills to navigate the world safely and successfully. By putting time and effort into socializing your Basset Hound, you may help to create a well-rounded, well-adjusted canine friend who is comfortable and happy in a variety of situations.

Curbing Excessive Barking and Howling

One of the most unique aspects of the Basset Hound is their vocal temperament, with their deep, resonant barks and howls being a source of both love and possible annoyance for their owners. While this vocalness is a natural and vital way of communication for Basset Hounds, excessive or improper barking and wailing can become a behavioral issue that requires careful supervision and training.

Basset Hounds are known to utilize their voices to express a variety of emotions and wants, from alerting potential predators or exciting stimuli to simply indicating their desire for attention or fun. Understanding the underlying causes of your Basset Hound's vocalizations is the first step in properly managing and reducing any excessive or undesired behaviors.

One major trigger for excessive barking and howling in Basset Hounds is boredom or lack of mental and physical activity. These hounds were originally developed for hunting, and their strong prey drive and scent-tracking talents can push them to vocalize when they are not supplied with suitable outlets for their energy and instincts. Ensuring that your Basset Hound has adequate daily exercise, meaningful playtime, and enrichment activities can help to minimize the frequency and intensity of their barking and wailing.

Separation anxiety can also be a contributing factor to excessive vocalizations in Basset Hounds. These friendly dogs often build close relationships with their human families and may get sad when left alone for extended periods. Implementing incremental desensitization and counterconditioning strategies, as well as giving your Basset Hound suitable coping mechanisms, such as puzzle toys or peaceful music, will assist in relieving separation-related barking and wailing.

In some situations, Basset Hounds may engage in barking or howling as a means of seeking attention or resources, such as food or playing. In these cases, it's crucial to avoid unwittingly encouraging undesirable behavior by responding to your dog's vocalizations. Instead, encourage and reinforce your Basset Hound when they are calm and quiet, and refocus their attention to more positive, constructive activities.

When handling excessive barking and wailing in Basset Hounds, it's crucial to stay patient, consistent, and positive in your approach. Harsh or punishing training methods may simply exacerbate the issue, as they can further heighten your dog's stress and anxiety levels. Instead, focus on giving adequate opportunity for physical and cerebral stimulation, adopting effective desensitization and counterconditioning techniques, and continually rewarding and reinforcing quiet, calm behavior.

By recognizing the underlying reasons for your Basset Hound's vocalizations and adopting a complete, positive-reinforcement-based training strategy, you may help to limit excessive barking and howling, creating a more harmonious living environment for both you and your canine partner.

Preventing Jumping and Nipping Behaviors

Jumping and nipping are frequent behavioral concerns that Basset Hound owners may confront, particularly throughout the puppy and adolescent periods. While these behaviors may appear sweet or harmless when your Basset Hound is tiny, they can rapidly become undesired and even harmful as your dog becomes older and stronger. Addressing and preventing jumping and nipping habits involves a proactive, persistent approach focused on positive reinforcement and good socialization.

Jumping up on people, whether to greet them or seek attention, is a normal habit among Basset Hounds, as they are often anxious to socialize with their human family members. However, this habit can become problematic, as it can lead to inadvertent scratches, knocked-over guests, and a general lack of control over your dog's actions.

To avoid and address jumping, it's crucial to continually reinforce the "four on the floor" rule, rewarding your Basset Hound with praise and goodies anytime all four paws remain on the ground. When your dog does jump up, instantly turn away or cross your arms, denying them the attention they seek. Redirect their energy to a more positive habit, such as sitting or lying down, and then reward them for the desired action.

Nipping, or playful biting, is another common issue that Basset Hound owners may confront, particularly during the puppy stage when teething and exploring behaviors are at their highest. While Basset Hounds may not aim to cause harm, their sharp puppy teeth can nonetheless inflict painful nips and bites, especially on tiny children or elderly adults.

To manage nipping, it's vital to redirect your Basset Hound's biting inclinations to appropriate chew toys and offer them many opportunities for constructive, supervised play. When your dog attempts to nip, forcefully shout "no" or "ouch," then instantly shift your attention by turning away or walking away. This teaches your Basset Hound that nipping behavior results in the loss of desirable engagement and reinforcement.

In addition to direct teaching tactics, adequate socializing is also crucial to preventing jumping and nipping habits in Basset Hounds. Exposing your dog to a variety of people, animals, and situations, while reinforcing calm, courteous interactions can assist in increasing their confidence and impulse control, minimizing the risk of these unwanted behaviors.

It's vital to note that, as with any training endeavor, patience and consistency are crucial when tackling jumping and nipping in Basset Hounds. These behaviors can be deeply established, and it may take time and practice to effectively modify them.

Celebrate little triumphs, change your technique as appropriate, and get the help of a professional dog trainer if you experience chronic obstacles.

By proactively addressing and preventing jumping and nipping behaviors through positive reinforcement, redirection, and proper socialization, you can help to ensure that your Basset Hound grows into a well-mannered, respectful companion, capable of safely and confidently interacting with people and other animals.

Chapter Seven

Advanced Obedience and Tricks

Teaching Complex Commands and Tricks

Beyond the core obedience instructions, teaching your Basset Hound more complicated talents and tricks can give a pleasant and stimulating experience for both you and your canine friend. These advanced training exercises not only demonstrate your dog's intelligence and trainability but also serve to keep their mind stimulated and improve the link between you.

One of the primary advantages of teaching complex commands and tricks to your Basset Hound is the possibility for enhanced involvement and problem-solving. These hounds, with their independent personality and excellent sense of smell, can occasionally become bored or disinterested in basic obedience training. By introducing more hard and rewarding exercises, you can tap into your Basset Hound's inherent interest and motivation, keeping them actively engaged and eager to learn.

When teaching complex commands and tricks, it's important to start with a solid foundation in the basics, such as "sit," "stay," and "come." These foundational skills will serve as building blocks for more advanced training, providing your Basset Hound with the necessary confidence and understanding to tackle new challenges.

Some examples of complex commands and tricks you can teach your Basset Hound include:

1. **"Spin" or "Turn":** This trick involves your Basset Hound whirling in a full circle, either clockwise or counterclockwise, on cue.

2. **"Shake" or "High Five":** Teaching your Basset Hound to extend their paw, either for a handshake or a high-five, can be a charming and adaptable trick.

3. **"Weave":** This command involves your Basset Hound weaving between a sequence of vertical objects, such as cones or poles, exhibiting their agility and response to your guidance.

4. **"Fetch" or "Retrieve":** Expanding on the fundamental "come" order, you can teach your Basset Hound to retrieve a specific object, such as a ball or toy, and bring it back to you.

When presenting these more sophisticated commands and tricks, be patient and break the training down into small, achievable chunks. Use positive reinforcement, such as food, praise, and play, to reward your Basset Hound for each successful effort, progressively increasing the challenge as they display mastery of the ability.

It's also crucial to personalize the training to your Basset Hound's specific learning style and disposition. Some dogs may thrive at particular types of tricks, while others may require more time and effort. Remain flexible and adaptable in your approach, and be prepared to change the training to keep your Basset Hound involved and motivated.

In addition to the mental stimulation and stronger bond, teaching difficult commands and tricks can also have practical benefits for your Basset Hound. Skills like "spin" or "weave" can be valuable for obedience competitions or agility training, while "fetch" and "retrieve" can come in handy during outdoor adventures or when playing interactive games.

By challenging your Basset Hound with advanced training, you not only boost their obedience and problem-solving skills but also offer them a satisfying and meaningful experience that can last a lifetime.

Incorporating Agility Training

Agility training is an interesting and rewarding sport that can bring several benefits for your Basset Hound, from developing their physical fitness to boosting their confidence and building the link between you and your canine partner.

While Basset Hounds may not be the first breed that springs to mind when considering agility training, these friendly, low-to-the-ground hounds may flourish in this sport with the appropriate approach and adjustments. Agility training can be particularly helpful for Basset Hounds, as it gives them much-needed physical and mental stimulation, helps to channel their natural hunting impulses, and offers a joyful, satisfying outlet for their energy and curiosity.

When introducing your Basset Hound to agility training, it's essential to start with a solid foundation in basic obedience commands, such as "sit," "stay," and "come." These skills will serve as the building blocks for more advanced agility exercises, providing your dog with the confidence and responsiveness needed to navigate the various obstacles and challenges.

One of the important concerns when introducing agility training into your Basset Hound's schedule is the necessity for customized or adapted equipment. Due to their unusual physical qualities, notably their low size and long backs, Basset Hounds may require specialized jumps, obstacles, and surfaces that accommodate their build and limit the danger of harm.

Work together with a skilled agility trainer or veterinarian to establish a safe and acceptable training plan for your Basset Hound. This may mean employing lower hurdles, broader contact zones, and other adaptations to the regular agility course to ensure your dog's comfort and well-being.

In addition to the physical benefits of agility training, this sport can also provide tremendous cerebral stimulation and enrichment for your Basset Hound. The need to navigate a variety of obstacles, respond to your cues, and problem-solve their way through the course can assist in keeping your dog involved, focused, and eager to learn.

As with any training attempt, patience and good reinforcement are crucial when teaching agility to your Basset Hound. Break down the training into short, achievable steps, and be sure to treat your dog generously for their efforts, whether they finish the course successfully or simply display a willingness to engage with the equipment.

It's important to understand that, while agility can be a highly satisfying sport for many Basset Hounds, it's not a one-size-fits-all pursuit. Some Basset Hounds may be more passionate and naturally oriented towards agility, while others may be less interested or even afraid. Respect your dog's comfort levels and be prepared to adapt the training plan as needed to provide a good, joyful experience for both you and your canine partner.

By introducing agility training into your Basset Hound's schedule, you can provide them with a unique and stimulating outlet for their physical and cerebral energy, all while building the link between you and your beloved hound.

Engaging in Scent Work and Nose Games

Harnessing the wonderful olfactory abilities of the Basset Hound through scent training and nose games may be a tremendously enjoyable and fulfilling hobby for both you and your canine partner. These hounds were originally selected for their remarkable sense of smell and tracking ability, and engaging them in scent-based exercises can assist in channeling their natural inclinations, provide cerebral stimulation, and enhance the link between you and your dog.

Scent work, often known as nose work, is a fast-emerging sport and training discipline that capitalizes on a dog's intrinsic ability to identify and track specific aromas. In a normal scent work activity, your Basset Hound is entrusted with detecting a hidden target odor, such as essential oils or certain food items, inside a predetermined search area. As your dog successfully detects the smell and marks its location, they are rewarded with praise, treats, or continuous access to the search.

One of the key benefits of introducing scent work into your Basset Hound's training schedule is the opportunity for mental stimulation and problem-solving. These hounds are naturally driven to follow their noses, and the challenge of discovering a hidden target can offer them a gratifying and fascinating pastime. As your Basset Hound continues through the numerous scent training exercises, they will build their olfactory skills, attention, and confidence, further improving their innate aptitude.

In addition to traditional scent work instruction, you can also engage your Basset Hound in several nose games and enrichment activities that rely on their extraordinary sense of smell. These can include:

1. Hide-and-Seek: Hiding your Basset Hound's favorite goodies or toys around the house or yard and challenging them to use their nose to locate the concealed items.

2. Snuffle Mats: Provide your Basset Hound with a specially made mat or box filled with various textured fabrics and hide treats or kibble between the folds, encouraging them to use their nose to look for the hidden prizes.

3. Scent Trails: Laying a trail of your Basset Hound's favorite treats or scented objects and guiding them to follow the trail, rewarding them when they reach the end.

When introducing your Basset Hound to scent training and nose games, it's vital to start with simple, low-stress exercises and progressively raise the complexity as your dog exhibits proficiency and confidence. Positive reinforcement, in the form of treats, praise, and continuing access to the search, is vital to keeping your Basset Hound engaged and motivated throughout the process.

It's crucial to remember that, while most Basset Hounds will joyfully embrace scent exercises and nose games, some may require more time and care to overcome any early hesitance or distraction. Respect your dog's comfort levels, be prepared to alter the training technique as needed, and always prioritize creating a pleasant, enjoyable experience for both you and your canine companion.

By combining scent work and nose games into your Basset Hound's training and enrichment activities, you can tap into their innate abilities, offer them mental stimulation, and develop a deeper, more meaningful link between you and your beloved hound.

Chapter Eight

Enrichment and Mental Stimulation

Providing Appropriate Toys and Chews

Basset Hounds, with their independent personality and high energy levels, require a range of enrichment activities and toys to keep them physically and mentally active. Providing your Basset Hound with proper toys and chews will not only prevent boredom and destructive tendencies but also contribute to their overall well-being and improve the link between you and your canine partner.

One of the most crucial considerations when purchasing toys and chews for your Basset Hound is their size and chewing power. These low-to-the-ground hounds have strong jaws and a tendency for determined chewing, so it's crucial to find robust, appropriate-sized products that can endure their excitement. Avoid small toys or chews that could provide a choking hazard, and steer clear of products made of substandard materials that may break apart or splinter, potentially inflicting internal damage.

Some fantastic toy options for Basset Hounds include:

1. Puzzle toys: Interactive puzzle feeders, snuffle mats, and treat-dispensing toys that test your Basset Hound's problem-solving skills and provide cerebral stimulation.

2. Plush toys: Durable, high-quality plush toys that can survive the demands of active play and give a comforting source of enrichment.

3. Rubber or nylon chews: Indestructible chew toys, such as Kongs or Nylabones, that satisfy your Basset Hound's natural chewing tendencies while improving oral health.

4. Rope toys: Sturdy, braided rope toys that allow your Basset Hound to engage in tug-of-war and other interactive play.

When purchasing toys and chews, it's crucial to consider your Basset Hound's specific tastes and demands. Some dogs may gravitate towards more interactive, puzzle-style toys, while others may prefer simple plush toys or chews. Observe your Basset Hound's behavior and interests, and be prepared to experiment with several sorts of enrichment to determine what resonates best with your canine buddy.

In addition to giving proper toys and chews, it's vital to ensure that your Basset Hound has adequate opportunities for play and exercise. These high-energetic hounds require regular physical activity, such as daily walks, playtime in a secure, fenced-in area, and interactive games, to help channel their energy and prevent boredom-related behavioral concerns.

Engaging your Basset Hound in interactive play with their toys and chews can also serve as a great bonding experience. Set out devoted playtime each day, where you can actively participate in tug-of-war, fetch, or hide-and-seek activities, rewarding your dog's engagement with praise, rewards, and continuous play.

It's crucial to note that, while toys and chews can provide a useful source of enrichment, they should not be utilized as a substitute for human engagement and training. Basset Hounds are highly social animals and thrive on the attention and guidance of their human family members. Ensure that your Basset Hound's toy and chew-based enrichment are balanced with regular exercise, training, and quality time spent together.

By providing your Basset Hound with a variety of appropriate, durable toys and chews, and incorporating them into your daily routine, you can help to meet their physical and mental needs, prevent boredom and destructive behaviors, and strengthen the bond between you and your beloved canine companion.

Introducing Clicker Training

Clicker training is a highly successful, positive-reinforcement-based training method that can be a helpful supplement to your Basset Hound's enrichment and mental stimulation schedule. This technique, which involves a small, handheld gadget that creates a characteristic "click" sound, can assist in enhancing your dog's reactivity, focus, and overall trainability, while also providing a pleasant, engaging pastime that improves the link between you and your canine partner.

The foundation of clicker training lies in the idea of operant conditioning, where desired behaviors are rewarded through the use of a distinct, constant marker (the clicker) and a reward. The clicker provides a precise, immediate manner to convey to your Basset Hound that they have executed the correct action, which is subsequently followed by a treat or other positive reinforcement.

One of the key benefits of clicker training for Basset Hounds is the way it taps into their inherent interest and problem-solving talents. These hounds, with their independent personality and excellent sense of smell, can occasionally become bored or disinterested in typical training methods. Clicker training, on the other hand, encourages your Basset Hound to engage actively with you, as they learn to anticipate the click and the accompanying reward for their desirable behaviors.

Additionally, the clicker's precision and consistency can be particularly effective for training Basset Hounds, as these dogs may respond better to the definite, rapid feedback provided by the clicker, rather than more subjective verbal cues or praise.

When introducing clicker training to your Basset Hound, it's vital to start by "charging the clicker" — a process that entails connecting the click sound with a reward or other positive reinforcement until your dog associates the two. Once your Basset Hound understands the concept of the clicker, you can begin adding it into your training sessions, using it to mark and reward desired behaviors, like sitting, making eye contact, or doing simple tricks.

As your Basset Hound becomes more skilled with clicker training, you can progressively introduce increasingly complex instructions and actions, always breaking them down into smaller, manageable steps and praising your dog's progress with the clicker and goodies. This strategy not only helps to retain your Basset Hound's involvement and interest but also allows you to fine-tune their knowledge and execution of the desired actions.

In addition to its training benefits, clicker work can also act as a great source of mental stimulation and enrichment for your Basset Hound. The challenge of mastering new abilities and the sense of accomplishment that comes with earning the clicker click and reward may be immensely enjoyable for these bright, food-motivated hounds.

When implementing clicker training into your Basset Hound's routine, be patient, consistent, and adaptable. Some dogs may take to the strategy more readily than others, so be prepared to adapt your approach as needed to ensure a good, joyful experience for both you and your canine buddy.

By using the power of clicker training, you can not only boost your Basset Hound's obedience and trainability but also give them a gratifying, psychologically engaging pastime that enhances the link between you and your beloved hound.

Maintaining Physical and Mental Fitness

Ensuring the total physical and mental fitness of your Basset Hound is vital for their well-being, longevity, and quality of life. These low-to-the-ground hounds, with their distinct physical traits and inclination for autonomous tendencies, require a well-rounded approach to exercise and enrichment to maintain optimal health and pleasure.

Physical Fitness:

Basset Hounds, despite their diminutive stature and relatively low energy levels compared to some other breeds, still require regular exercise to maintain their physical fitness and prevent health complications. A sedentary lifestyle can lead to weight gain, musculoskeletal difficulties, and other potentially significant medical conditions. To keep your Basset Hound physically fit, add the following to their regular routine:

1. **Moderate daily walks**: Aim for at least two 20-30 minute walks per day, changing the time and intensity based on your Basset Hound's age, fitness level, and environmental circumstances.

2. **Supervised playtime**: Provide your Basset Hound with access to a secure, fenced-in area where they can engage in enthusiastic play, such as fetch or tug-of-war, under your careful supervision.

3. Low-impact activities: Consider incorporating low-impact exercises, such as swimming or restricted leash-free hiking, to help build your Basset Hound's muscles and joints without putting excessive strain on their body.

4. Weight management: Monitor your Basset Hound's weight and change their diet and exercise program as needed to maintain a healthy, lean body condition.

Mental Fitness:

In addition to physical fitness, preserving the mental well-being of your Basset Hound is as crucial. These bright, scent-driven hounds require continuous mental stimulation to prevent boredom, anxiety, and the development of undesired behavioral difficulties.

1. Enrichment toys and activities: Provide your Basset Hound with a range of interactive toys, puzzle feeders, and scent-based games to test their problem-solving skills and activate their innate hunting instincts.

2. Training and skill-building: Regularly practice obedience commands, teach new tricks, and include clicker training or other positive-reinforcement-based methods to keep your Basset Hound's mind engaged and challenged.

3. Socialization and exploration: Expose your Basset Hound to new locations, people, and experiences in a pleasant, regulated manner to help increase their confidence and lessen fear.

4. Cognitive exercises: Engage your Basset Hound in activities that develop their senses and problem-solving abilities, such as hide-and-seek, food puzzles, or scent work.

It's important to know that, as Basset Hounds age, their activity and enrichment needs may change. Older Basset Hounds may require more moderate, low-impact exercises, as well as additional cerebral stimulation to preserve their physical and cognitive well-being. Consult with your veterinarian to build a personalized fitness and enrichment regimen that suits your Basset Hound's demands at every stage of your life.

By addressing the physical and mental fitness of your Basset Hound, you may help to ensure their long-term health, prevent the development of behavioral difficulties, and establish a strong, enduring link between you and your cherished canine partner.

Chapter Nine

Training Techniques for Senior Basset Hounds

Adapting Training Methods for Older Dogs

As Basset Hounds age, their training and enrichment needs may alter, needing a thoughtful and adaptive approach to ensure their continuing well-being and quality of life. Older Basset Hounds bring a wealth of knowledge and wisdom, but they also have unique physical and cognitive obstacles that demand adaptations to typical training approaches.

One of the key considerations while teaching older Basset Hounds is their reduced physical capabilities. These older hounds may endure joint pain, limited mobility, and diminished stamina, making traditional high-intensity training or prolonged exercise sessions potentially unpleasant and painful. To accommodate these changes, it's necessary to adapt your training strategy to focus on low-impact, moderate exercises that maintain your Basset Hound's physical condition without creating undue stress or discomfort.

When working with a senior Basset Hound, integrate more frequent, shorter training sessions, and favor activities that encourage mental stimulation over physical exertion. This may involve clicker training, scent work, and interactive puzzle toys, which engage your dog's cognitive abilities without demanding undue physical effort.

Additionally, be careful of the setting in which you perform your training sessions. Opt for well-padded, non-slip surfaces to provide support and traction for your senior Basset Hound, and avoid training on slippery floors or uneven terrain that could increase the danger of falls or injury.

Another crucial element to consider when changing your training methods for elderly Basset Hounds is their probable deterioration in sensory abilities, such as hearing or vision loss. These changes can impair your dog's reaction to traditional verbal cues or hand gestures, necessitating the usage of alternate communication methods.

Incorporate the use of visual aids, such as hand signals or target sticks, to supplement or substitute spoken directions, and be patient and attentive to your senior Basset Hound's capacity to perceive and comprehend your instructions. Additionally, begin training in low-distraction surroundings to avoid external stimuli that could further strain your dog's senses.

It's also crucial to note that senior Basset Hounds may take more time and effort to acquire new skills or retain previously taught commands. Be patient, break down training into smaller, achievable steps, and applaud even the tiniest of triumphs to retain your senior dog's motivation and confidence.

When dealing with a senior Basset Hound, it's crucial to contact your veterinarian to ensure that any training or enrichment activities are acceptable for your dog's individual health and physical condition. Your vet may also be able to provide specific information or ideas on how to best assist your senior Basset Hound's training and overall well-being.

By customizing your training methods to match the special demands and limits of your senior Basset Hound, you may assist in preserving their cognitive stimulation, physical health, and general quality of life, while building the link between you and your cherished canine partner.

Addressing Age-Related Challenges

As Basset Hounds mature in age, they may experience a variety of physical and cognitive issues that require deliberate management and care. Understanding and managing these age-related difficulties can help to assure the continued well-being and comfort of your senior Basset Hound, letting them enjoy their golden years to the fullest.

One of the biggest concerns with aging Basset Hounds is the increasing risk of joint and mobility disorders, such as arthritis, hip and elbow dysplasia, and intervertebral disc disease. These disorders can cause pain, stiffness, and limited movement, making it vital to work closely with your veterinarian to design an effective treatment plan.

This may involve the use of joint supplements, anti-inflammatory drugs, and low-impact exercise programs to assist ease discomfort and maintain your senior Basset Hound's range of motion. Additionally, giving your dog comfortable, supportive bedding and exploring the use of assistive devices, such as ramps or stairs, can help to increase their mobility and lessen the strain on their aging joints.

Another common age-related challenge faced by senior Basset Hounds is the potential for cognitive decline, often referred to as canine cognitive dysfunction or "dog dementia." This condition can manifest in a variety of ways, including disorientation, changes in sleep-wake cycles, and alterations in learning and memory.

To address the cognitive decline in your senior Basset Hound, work closely with your veterinarian to rule out any underlying medical concerns and explore appropriate treatment options, which may include medications, dietary supplements, and environmental enrichment tactics.

Ensuring that your senior Basset Hound maintains a constant routine, with familiar surroundings and a predictable schedule, can assist in creating a sense of comfort and stability, decreasing the chance of confusion or anxiety. Additionally, engaging your dog in mentally challenging activities, like food puzzles, scent work, and clicker training, can assist in maintaining their cognitive function and prevent the course of cognitive loss.

As Basset Hounds mature, they may also become more prone to sensory problems, such as hearing or vision loss. These changes can impair your dog's ability to traverse their environment, respond to cues, and engage with their surroundings. Adapting your environment to these sensory changes, such as employing visual cues or providing olfactory advice, can help to ensure your senior Basset Hound's safety and comfort.

It's crucial to know that elderly Basset Hounds may also be more prone to medical disorders, such as dental disease, heart problems, or kidney troubles. Maintaining regular veterinary check-ups and promptly treating any health problems will help to prevent or manage these age-related diseases, guaranteeing your senior dog's general well-being.

By addressing the special problems experienced by senior Basset Hounds, you may assist in maintaining their quality of life, support their physical and cognitive needs, and develop a strong, meaningful link with your beloved canine partner during their golden years.

Keeping Your Senior Basset Hound Engaged

As Basset Hounds hit their senior years, it's crucial to find ways to keep them engaged, mentally occupied, and enjoying a great quality of life. While age-related changes may demand adaptations to their exercise and training regimes, there are several ways to enrich and maintain your senior dog's well-being.

One of the essential tactics for keeping your senior Basset Hound motivated is to continue their training and skill-building activities but with suitable adaptations. While high-intensity physical exercises may no longer be suitable, you can focus on mild, low-impact training that challenges your dog's cognitive talents.

Clicker training, for example, can be a fantastic tool for senior Basset Hounds, as it provides rapid feedback and rewards, helping to retain their focus and motivation. Incorporate simple tasks, such as "shake," "spin," or "touch," and break down the training into tiny, achievable steps to fit your older dog's speed and physical ability.

Scent work and nose games can also be a terrific way to stimulate your senior Basset Hound's innate hunting instincts and problem-solving skills. Set up basic scent trails or hide-and-seek activities, rewarding your dog's efforts with praise and food. These cognitive exercises can assist in stimulating your senior Basset Hound's intellect and create a sense of purpose and success.

In addition to training and cognitive exercises, integrating enrichment toys and puzzles into your senior Basset Hound's daily routine can also assist in keeping them engaged and mentally occupied. Look for interactive feeders, snuffle mats, or treat-dispensing toys that challenge your dog's problem-solving talents without needing undue physical work.

Regular interaction and exposure to new experiences can also be helpful for elderly Basset Hounds, as these activities can assist in retaining their confidence and cognitive flexibility. Arrange supervised playdates with well-socialized canine buddies, or take your senior dog on field trips to pet-friendly establishments or parks, where they can safely engage with new people and situations.

It's important to remember that, as Basset Hounds age, their exercise and activity needs may fluctuate. While keeping physical fitness is critical, it's crucial to balance your senior dog's enrichment with enough rest and recovery time. Provide your senior Basset Hound with comfortable, supportive bedding and allow them to decide the pace and duration of their daily activities.

Additionally, pay attention to your senior Basset Hound's body language and energy levels, and be prepared to adapt your enrichment and engagement tactics as needed. Some days, your senior dog may prefer a peaceful, relaxed setting, while on others, they may be anxious to participate in more active, exciting activities.

By keeping your senior Basset Hound engaged, mentally occupied, and socially connected, you may assist in maintaining their cognitive function, physical well-being, and general quality of life during their golden years. This, in turn, can increase the link between you and your cherished canine companion, offering a fulfilling and meaningful experience for both of you.

Chapter Ten

Reinforcing and Troubleshooting Training

Successful training for your Basset Hound doesn't end once your dog has learned the fundamental instructions. Maintaining and reinforcing those behaviors via constant repetition is crucial to ensuring your Basset Hound's training sticks. Additionally, being prepared to handle any training regressions or problems that may develop can help you keep your dog on the right track. This final chapter will discuss the important parts of reinforcing your Basset Hound's training and solutions for handling potential setbacks.

Establishing a Consistent Training Routine

Consistency is the foundation of efficient dog training, and this is especially important when working with a stubborn breed like the Basset Hound. Establishing a consistent training regimen can assist your Basset Hound in comprehending your expectations and preserving the traits you've worked hard to inculcate.

Start by setting aside specific training sessions at the same time each day. Aim for numerous short, frequent sessions rather than one long one. This keeps your Basset Hound involved and allows you to leave on a positive note before they become bored or frustrated. Stick to the same location, directives, and training techniques to establish a predictable learning environment.

During these sessions, focus on practicing the basic commands your Basset Hound has already learned, such as sit, stay, come, and heel. Weave in new techniques or sophisticated commands as you see appropriate, but don't forget the fundamentals. Repetition is crucial for consolidating your Basset Hound's training.

Consistency should also extend beyond your scheduled training sessions. Incorporate training into your daily contacts with your Basset Hound, such as asking them to sit and wait before meals or to come when called during playing. The more opportunities you allow for your Basset Hound to practice their training, the more established the behaviors will become.

Keep in mind that your Basset Hound may thrive at certain commands but struggle with others. Adjust your training program to focus more on the regions that need the most development. With time and patience, you'll start to see gains across the board.

Establishing a consistent training schedule takes dedication, but it pays off in a well-trained, attentive Basset Hound. Your dog will thrive on predictability and feel more confident in their talents.

Rewarding and Praising Your Basset Hound

Positive reinforcement is the foundation of efficient dog training, and it's especially crucial when working with a breed like the Basset Hound, which may be independent and difficult at times. Rewarding and praising your Basset Hound for their triumphs is vital for reinforcing the behaviors you want to see.

During training sessions, be generous with the usage of high-value prizes, such as little pieces of cooked chicken, hot dog, or your Basset Hound's favorite foods. These rewards should be something your dog appreciates and perceives as a special treat, not their ordinary food. Pair the food reward with passionate praise, petting, and attention to develop a positive link with the desired behavior.

As your Basset Hound develops in their training, you may progressively phase out the food rewards and rely more on praise and play as the major reinforcement. A simple "Good job!" or "Yay, you did it!" paired with an enthusiastic pat or game of tug can be just as successful in reinforcing your Basset Hound's efforts.

It's vital to time your rewards and praise right. The incentive should come soon after your Basset Hound accomplishes the desired behavior, so they understand exactly what they're being praised for. Avoid delayed satisfaction, as your Basset Hound may grow confused about which activity led to the prize.

In addition to rewarding during training sessions, search for opportunities to praise and thank your Basset Hound throughout the day. Catch them being good and reinforce appropriate behaviors, such as gently relaxing in their bed or welcoming you graciously at the entrance. This helps reinforce the positive association and encourages your Basset Hound to repeat those activities.

Be wary not to overdo the rewards, as this might lead to your Basset Hound becoming dependent on them or only doing behaviors when a treat is involved. Gradually lessen the frequency of food rewards while retaining the passionate praise and attention.

Rewarding and praising your Basset Hound frequently and appropriately will not only reinforce their training but also enhance the link between you. Your Basset Hound will learn to work for your acceptance and affection, which may be a powerful motivation.

Identifying and Addressing Training Regressions

Even the best-trained Basset Hounds can undergo occasional training regressions, where previously taught behaviors start to weaken or disappear. This is a typical component of the training process and should be expected, especially during times of stress, excitement, or changes in routine.

The first step in treating training regressions is to determine the underlying cause. Common factors for Basset Hound training regressions include:

- **Changes in surroundings or routine**: Basset Hounds depend on consistency, and any big interruptions to their daily lives can drive them to revert to old habits.

- **Stress or anxiety**: Stressful events, such as a move, new family member, or veterinarian appointment, might cause your Basset Hound to become uncomfortable and struggle with their training.

- **Boredom or lack of exercise**: If your Basset Hound is not getting enough physical and mental stimulation, they may start to display undesired behaviors as a method to release pent-up energy.

- **Medical issues**: Underlying health problems, pain, or discomfort might contribute to training regressions since your Basset Hound may have trouble focusing or may be less eager to perform.

Once you've discovered the likely trigger, you can build a plan to address the issue and get your Basset Hound back on track.

If the regression is due to a change in environment or habit, try to reintroduce the training commands and expectations gradually. Go back to the basics, using high-value treats and plenty of praise to remind your Basset Hound of what's expected. Slowly re-introduce the new features while keeping the training sessions short and encouraging.

For stress-related regressions, focus on offering your Basset Hound with extra comfort, reassurance, and relaxing activities. This may include employing anxiety-reducing tools like pheromone diffusers, playing soothing music, or engaging in low-key activities like gentle brushing or nose work. Gradually restart training once your Basset Hound has had time to decompress.

If boredom or lack of exercise seems to be the reason, make sure you're providing your Basset Hound with appropriate physical and mental stimulation. Increase the amount and intensity of regular walks, integrate more playing and interactive toys, and consider trying new training techniques like clicker training or scent work to keep your Basset Hound involved.

In circumstances where a medical condition is suspected, it's crucial to have your Basset Hound evaluated by a veterinarian. Underlying pain or discomfort can make it harder for your dog to focus during training, so resolving any health concerns should be the main priority.

Lastly, be patient and persistent while correcting training regressions. It may take time and effort to get your Basset Hound back on track, but with consistency, positive reinforcement, and a little troubleshooting, you can overcome these momentary obstacles.

Remember, training is a continual process, and even the best-trained Basset Hounds will occasionally need a refresher. By being prepared to spot and solve training regressions, you'll be able to preserve your Basset Hound's skills and keep them well-behaved throughout their lives.

20 homemade food recipe ideas for Basset Hound with ingredients and preparation instructions

1. Beef and Sweet Potato Stew

Ingredients:

- 1 lb ground beef
- 2 medium sweet potatoes, peeled and diced
- 1 cup frozen peas
- 1 cup diced carrots
- 2 cups low-sodium beef broth
- 1 tsp dried thyme
- 1 tsp dried parsley
- 1/2 tsp ground turmeric

Preparation:

In a large pot, brown the ground beef over medium heat. Drain any excess fat. Add the sweet potatoes, peas, carrots, beef broth, thyme, parsley, and turmeric. Bring the mixture to a boil, then reduce heat and simmer for 30-40 minutes, or until the vegetables are tender. Allow to cool slightly before serving.

2. Chicken and Brown Rice Bowl

Ingredients:

- 1 lb boneless, skinless chicken breasts, cooked and diced
- 2 cups cooked brown rice
- 1 cup diced zucchini
- 1/2 cup diced bell peppers
- 2 tbsp chopped fresh parsley
- 1 tsp olive oil
- 1/4 tsp ground ginger

Preparation:

In a large bowl, combine the cooked chicken, brown rice, zucchini, bell peppers, parsley, olive oil, and ground ginger. Mix well to evenly distribute the ingredients. Serve warm or at room temperature.

3. Salmon and Quinoa Patties

Ingredients:

- 1 (15 oz) can wild-caught salmon, drained and flaked
- 1 cup cooked quinoa
- 1 egg, beaten
- 1/4 cup rolled oats
- 2 tbsp chopped fresh dill
- 1 tsp lemon zest
- 1/4 tsp sea salt

Preparation:

In a medium bowl, mix together the flaked salmon, quinoa, beaten egg, rolled oats, dill, lemon zest, and sea salt until well combined. Form the mixture into small patties, about 2-3 inches in diameter. Heat a nonstick skillet over medium heat and cook the patties for 3-4 minutes per side, or until golden brown.

4. Turkey and Vegetable Meatballs

Ingredients:

- 1 lb ground turkey
- 1 cup diced sweet potatoes
- 1/2 cup diced spinach
- 1/4 cup rolled oats
- 1 egg, beaten
- 1 tsp dried parsley
- 1/2 tsp garlic powder
- 1/4 tsp sea salt

Preparation:

Preheat your oven to 375°F (190°C). In a large bowl, combine the ground turkey, diced sweet potatoes, spinach, rolled oats, beaten egg, parsley, garlic powder, and sea salt. Mix until all the ingredients are well incorporated. Roll the mixture into small, bite-sized meatballs and place them on a baking sheet lined with parchment paper. Bake for 20-25 minutes, or until the meatballs are cooked through.

5. Beef and Barley Stew
Ingredients:

- 1 lb beef stew meat, cubed

- 1 cup pearl barley

- 2 cups diced carrots

- 1 cup diced celery

- 1 onion, diced

- 4 cups low-sodium beef broth

- 2 tbsp tomato paste

- 1 tsp dried thyme

- 1/2 tsp sea salt

Preparation:

In a large pot, combine the beef stew meat, pearl barley, carrots, celery, onion, beef broth, tomato paste, thyme, and sea salt. Bring the mixture to a boil, then reduce heat and simmer for 60-80 minutes, or until the beef and barley are tender. Adjust seasoning if needed.

6. Pumpkin and Oat Dog Biscuits
Ingredients:

- 1 cup whole wheat flour

- 1 cup rolled oats

- 1/2 cup canned pumpkin puree

- 1/4 cup unsweetened applesauce

- 1 egg

- 1 tsp ground cinnamon

Preparation:

Preheat your oven to 350°F (175°C). In a large bowl, mix together the whole wheat flour, rolled oats, pumpkin puree, applesauce, egg, and cinnamon until a dough forms. Roll the dough out to about 1/4-inch thickness and use cookie cutters to cut out desired shapes. Place the biscuits on a baking sheet lined with parchment paper. Bake for 20-25 minutes, or until the biscuits are golden brown and firm.

7. Chicken and Vegetable Stir-Fry
Ingredients:

- 1 lb boneless, skinless chicken breasts, diced

- 2 cups mixed frozen vegetables (e.g., broccoli, cauliflower, carrots)

- 1 cup cooked brown rice

- 2 tbsp low-sodium soy sauce

- 1 tsp sesame oil

- 1 tsp grated ginger

Preparation:

In a large skillet or wok, stir-fry the diced chicken over medium-high heat until cooked through, about 5-7 minutes. Add the frozen vegetables and continue cooking for an additional 5 minutes, or until the vegetables are tender. Stir in the cooked brown rice, soy sauce, sesame oil, and grated ginger. Mix well and serve warm.

8. Beef and Vegetable Casserole

Ingredients:

- 1 lb ground beef

- 2 cups diced potatoes

- 1 cup diced carrots

- 1 cup frozen peas

- 1 onion, diced

- 2 cups low-sodium beef broth

- 1 tsp dried thyme

- 1/2 tsp sea salt

Preparation:

Preheat your oven to 375°F (190°C). In a large oven-safe pot or casserole dish, brown the ground beef over medium heat. Drain any excess fat. Add the diced potatoes, carrots, frozen peas, and onion. Pour in the beef broth and stir in the dried thyme and sea salt. Cover the dish and bake for 45-60 minutes, or until the vegetables are tender.

9. Turkey and Sweet Potato Meatloaf

Ingredients:
- 1 lb ground turkey
- 1 cup shredded sweet potatoes
- 1/2 cup old-fashioned oats
- 1 egg, beaten
- 1/4 cup unsweetened applesauce
- 2 tbsp chopped fresh parsley
- 1 tsp garlic powder
- 1/2 tsp sea salt

Preparation:

Preheat your oven to 375°F (190°C). In a large bowl, combine the ground turkey, shredded sweet potatoes, oats, beaten egg, applesauce, parsley, garlic powder, and sea salt. Mix until all the ingredients are well incorporated. Transfer the mixture to a loaf pan and bake for 45-55 minutes, or until the meatloaf is cooked through. Allow it to cool slightly before slicing and serving.

10. Salmon and Quinoa Casserole

Ingredients:

- 1 (15 oz) can wild-caught salmon, drained and flaked
- 1 cup cooked quinoa
- 1 cup diced sweet potatoes
- 1/2 cup frozen peas
- 1/4 cup grated Parmesan cheese
- 2 tbsp chopped fresh dill
- 1 egg, beaten
- 1/4 tsp sea salt

Preparation:

Preheat your oven to 375°F (190°C). In a large bowl, combine the flaked salmon, cooked quinoa, diced sweet potatoes, frozen peas, Parmesan cheese, chopped dill, beaten egg, and sea salt. Mix well until all the ingredients are evenly distributed. Transfer the mixture to a baking dish and bake for 30-35 minutes, or until the casserole is heated through and the top is lightly browned.

11. Chicken and Brown Rice Stuffed Peppers
Ingredients:
- 4 bell peppers, halved and seeded
- 1 lb ground chicken
- 1 cup cooked brown rice
- 1 cup diced tomatoes
- 1/2 cup shredded cheddar cheese
- 2 tbsp chopped fresh basil
- 1 tsp garlic powder
- 1/4 tsp sea salt

Preparation:

Preheat your oven to 375°F (190°C). Place the bell pepper halves in a baking dish. In a large bowl, mix together the ground chicken, cooked brown rice, diced tomatoes, shredded cheddar cheese, chopped basil, garlic powder, and sea salt. Spoon the chicken and rice mixture into the bell pepper halves, packing it down gently. Bake for 35-40 minutes, or until the peppers are tender and the filling is cooked through.

12. Beef and Vegetable Stir-Fry with Cauliflower Rice

Ingredients:

- 1 lb beef sirloin, thinly sliced
- 2 cups mixed frozen vegetables (e.g., broccoli, carrots, snow peas)
- 1 head of cauliflower, riced
- 2 tbsp low-sodium soy sauce
- 1 tbsp sesame oil
- 1 tsp grated ginger

Preparation:

In a large skillet or wok, stir-fry the sliced beef over high heat until browned, about 5-7 minutes. Add the mixed frozen vegetables and continue cooking for an additional 5 minutes, or until the vegetables are tender. In a separate pan, sauté the riced cauliflower over medium heat until heated through, about 5 minutes. Stir the soy sauce, sesame oil, and grated ginger into the beef and vegetable mixture. Serve the stir-fry over the cauliflower rice.

13. Lamb and Sweet Potato Stew

Ingredients:
- 1 lb lamb stew meat, cubed
- 2 cups diced sweet potatoes
- 1 cup diced carrots
- 1 onion, diced
- 4 cups low-sodium beef or vegetable broth
- 2 tbsp tomato paste
- 1 tsp dried rosemary
- 1/2 tsp sea salt

Preparation:

In a large pot, combine the cubed lamb, diced sweet potatoes, carrots, onion, beef or vegetable broth, tomato paste, dried rosemary, and sea salt. Bring the mixture to a boil, then reduce heat and simmer for 60-80 minutes, or until the lamb and vegetables are tender. Adjust seasoning if needed.

14. Peanut Butter and Banana Dog Treats

Ingredients:
- 1 cup whole wheat flour
- 1/2 cup natural peanut butter
- 1 ripe banana, mashed
- 1 egg
- 1/4 cup water (as needed)

Preparation:

Preheat your oven to 350°F (175°C). In a large bowl, mix together the whole wheat flour, peanut butter, mashed banana, and egg until a dough forms. If the dough is too dry, add water 1 tablespoon at a time until it reaches the desired consistency. Roll the dough out to about 1/4-inch thickness and use cookie cutters to cut out desired shapes. Place the treats on a baking sheet lined with parchment paper. Bake for 20-25 minutes, or until the treats are golden brown and crispy.

15. Turkey and Vegetable Frittata

Ingredients:
- 6 eggs, beaten
- 1/2 lb ground turkey
- 1 cup diced zucchini
- 1/2 cup diced bell peppers
- 1/4 cup shredded cheddar cheese
- 2 tbsp chopped fresh parsley
- 1/4 tsp sea salt

Preparation:
Preheat your oven to 375°F (190°C). In a large oven-safe skillet, cook the ground turkey over medium heat until browned and cooked through. Drain any excess fat. Add the diced zucchini and bell peppers to the skillet and sauté for 5 minutes, or until the vegetables are slightly softened. In a

separate bowl, whisk the eggs and stir in the shredded cheddar cheese, chopped parsley, and sea salt. Pour the egg mixture over the turkey and vegetables in the skillet. Bake for 20-25 minutes, or until the frittata is set and lightly browned on top.

16. Beef and Barley Soup

Ingredients:
- 1 lb ground beef
- 1 cup pearl barley
- 4 cups low-sodium beef broth
- 2 cups diced carrots
- 1 cup diced celery
- 1 onion, diced
- 2 tbsp tomato paste
- 1 tsp dried thyme
- 1/2 tsp sea salt

Preparation:
In a large pot, brown the ground beef over medium heat. Drain any excess fat. Add the pearl barley,

beef broth, carrots, celery, onion, tomato paste, dried thyme, and sea salt. Bring the mixture to a boil, then reduce heat and simmer for 45-60 minutes, or until the barley and vegetables are tender.

17. Chicken and Veggie Meatballs

Ingredients:

- 1 lb ground chicken
- 1 cup diced sweet potatoes
- 1/2 cup diced broccoli
- 1/4 cup rolled oats
- 1 egg, beaten
- 2 tbsp chopped fresh basil
- 1 tsp garlic powder
- 1/4 tsp sea salt

Preparation:

Preheat your oven to 375°F (190°C). In a large bowl, mix together the ground chicken, diced sweet potatoes, broccoli, rolled oats, beaten egg, chopped basil, garlic powder, and sea salt until well combined. Roll the mixture into small, bite-sized meatballs and place them on a baking sheet lined with parchment paper. Bake for 20-25 minutes, or until the meatballs are cooked through.

18. Sardine and Quinoa Cakes
Ingredients:
- 1 (4.25 oz) can of sardines, drained and flaked
- 1 cup cooked quinoa
- 1 egg, beaten
- 1/4 cup rolled oats
- 2 tbsp chopped fresh parsley
- 1 tsp lemon zest
- 1/4 tsp sea salt

Preparation:
In a medium bowl, mix together the flaked sardines, cooked quinoa, beaten egg, rolled oats, chopped parsley, lemon zest, and sea salt until well combined. Form the mixture into small patties, about 2-3 inches in diameter. Heat a nonstick

skillet over medium heat and cook the cakes for 3-4 minutes per side, or until golden brown.

19. Beef and Sweet Potato Hash

Ingredients:

- 1 lb ground beef

- 2 cups diced sweet potatoes

- 1 cup diced bell peppers

- 1 onion, diced

- 2 tbsp chopped fresh cilantro

- 1 tsp ground cumin

- 1/2 tsp smoked paprika

- 1/4 tsp sea salt

Preparation:

In a large skillet, cook the ground beef over medium heat until browned and cooked through. Drain any excess fat. Add the diced sweet potatoes, bell peppers, and onion to the skillet. Cook for 15-20 minutes, stirring occasionally, until the vegetables are tender. Stir in the chopped cilantro, ground cumin, smoked paprika, and sea salt. Mix well and serve.

20. Pumpkin and Oat Breakfast Bites

Ingredients:

- 1 cup rolled oats
- 1/2 cup canned pumpkin puree
- 1/4 cup natural peanut butter
- 2 tbsp honey
- 1 tsp ground cinnamon

Preparation:

In a medium bowl, combine the rolled oats, pumpkin puree, peanut butter, honey, and ground cinnamon. Mix until all the ingredients are well incorporated. Using a small cookie scoop or spoon, form the mixture into bite-sized balls and place them on a baking sheet lined with parchment paper. Refrigerate for at least 30 minutes before serving.